GINGER ALLEN

Backyard Chickens on a Budget

Everything you need to know to start your flock without breaking the bank

Copyright © 2025 by Ginger Allen

All rights reserved. No part of this publication may be reproduced, stored or transmitted in any form or by any means, electronic, mechanical, photocopying, recording, scanning, or otherwise without written permission from the publisher. It is illegal to copy this book, post it to a website, or distribute it by any other means without permission.

Ginger Allen asserts the moral right to be identified as the author of this work.

Ginger Allen has no responsibility for the persistence or accuracy of URLs for external or third-party Internet Websites referred to in this publication and does not guarantee that any content on such Websites is, or will remain, accurate or appropriate.

Designations used by companies to distinguish their products are often claimed as trademarks. All brand names and product names used in this book and on its cover are trade names, service marks, trademarks and registered trademarks of their respective owners. The publishers and the book are not associated with any product or vendor mentioned in this book. None of the companies referenced within the book have endorsed the book.

First edition

This book was professionally typeset on Reedsy.
Find out more at reedsy.com

Contents

	Introduction	1
1	Preparing for Your Chicks	4
2	Buying Your Chicks	8
3	Caring for Chicks Indoors	14
4	Transitioning to the Coop	20
5	When to Expect Eggs	24
6	Flock Planning for Long-Term Success	28
7	Health Checks & Common Ailments	33
8	Keep Growing With Your Flock	39
9	Resources	42
	About the Author	44

Introduction

I still remember the first time we brought home a box of baby chicks. Their tiny peeps, wobbly legs, and boundless curiosity melted my heart faster than I could say "What have we gotten ourselves into?" I had done the research—*so much* research. I'd read every blog, watched countless hours of YouTube, and let's just say we may have binged a few too many episodes of *Homestead Rescue* (Raney, 2016–present) for our own good. We had this dream of doing things ourselves, even if it meant a little bootstrapping.

We started our journey on a modest 2-acre property—inside city limits, no less. My husband built our coop entirely from scratch with free wood we scavenged from old fences on Facebook Marketplace. I'm not saying you have to go that route, but for us, it felt like the start of something *real*. Of course, in true first-time chicken-keeping fashion, we ended up with an accidental rooster. Thankfully, all of our neighbors had chickens (and roosters) of their own, so he fit right in.

That first batch taught us a lot—mostly what *not* to do. The next time around, we got smart and stuck with sex-linked and autosexed breeds to avoid any surprise crowing. Don't worry, we'll cover all of that in this book.

We're still relatively new to the homesteading world—officially starting our journey in 2024—but let me tell you, every single day is a learning experience. We spent *months* in analysis paralysis, convinced we needed to know *everything* before we started. Spoiler alert: you'll never know everything. Jumping in is part of the process. That's how we grow.

And here's something even more important: **failure is part of the process, too.** Every time something doesn't go as planned—whether it's a coop that leaks, a chick that needs extra care, or a garden that flops—it's not really a failure. It's just an opportunity to learn, adapt, and do better next time. Those "failures" are how you become a better chicken tender, a more resilient homesteader, and a stronger, more confident version of yourself.

And now? We're building our dream home on a large property out in the country, making those wild homesteading dreams come true—one project (and chicken) at a time.

I wrote this book because I wish something like it had existed when I started. A down-to-earth, honest guide written by someone who's in the trenches, figuring it out right alongside you. Whether you're building a backyard coop from scratch, buying your chicks from the local feed store, or dreaming about country acreage while living in a suburban neighborhood—this guide is for you.

Chickens are for everyone. You don't need a farm or a big budget. You just need a little space, some basic supplies, and a whole lot of love. These birds are easy to keep, fun to watch, and provide your family with delicious, protein-rich eggs. But here's the kicker: they're also a gateway. Before you know it, you'll be fermenting your own sourdough, planting a food garden, and eyeing goats, pigs, or maybe even a milk cow.

INTRODUCTION

Backyard chickens are the beginning of something beautiful—and beautifully simple.

Let's get started.

1

Preparing for Your Chicks

Before you bring home those fluffy little peepers, it's important to have their new home ready. Just like babies, chicks need a safe, warm space where they can eat, sleep, and grow without stress. But don't worry—you don't need a Pinterest-worthy setup or a ton of money. With a little creativity (and maybe a repurposed storage bin or two), you can give your chicks everything they need.

The Brooder: Your Chick Nursery

A brooder is simply a warm, protected space for chicks to live during their first few weeks. You can absolutely buy a fancy brooder—but you don't need to. Many chicken keepers (myself included) start with things like plastic storage totes, large cardboard boxes, or even repurposed kiddie pools.

My Setup: I've personally had great success using a pop-up dog kennel as my brooder. It's portable, breathable, easy to clean, and roomy enough for growing chicks. I just add hemp bedding on the bottom, a heat source, and secure the sides to keep everything safe and cozy.

What You'll Need:

- Brooder box (plastic tub, cardboard box, dog kennel, etc.)
- Heat source (brooder plate or heat lamp—see below)
- Bedding (pine shavings, hemp, or puppy pads for early days)
- Chick-sized feeder and waterer
- Thermometer to monitor temps

For day-by-day care and routines, we'll walk through everything in Chapter 3.

Heat Source Options

You'll need to keep the brooder warm—starting around 95°F and reducing by 5°F each week. You can choose from:

- **Heat Lamps** – Affordable and easy to find, but pose a fire risk and can overheat the entire brooder.
- **Brooder Plates** – Mimic a mother hen, safer, and chicks can regulate warmth by going under it. They heat bodies—not the air.

We personally prefer brooder plates for peace of mind and safety.

Bedding Basics

- **Days 1–3**: Use puppy pads or paper towels. This helps prevent chicks from eating bedding and makes it easy to monitor droppings.
- **After Day 3**: Transition to pine shavings or hemp bedding (never cedar—it's toxic!).

Why hemp? It's more absorbent and controls odor better than pine.

It's low-dust, compostable, and needs changing less often, which helps balance out the upfront cost.

Brooder Location

Pick a quiet, draft-free area that's safe from pets and near a power outlet. Good options include:

- Spare bathrooms
- Laundry rooms
- Garages (if temperature-controlled)

Avoid cold basements or outdoor sheds in early spring.

Supplies Checklist

Here's a basic list of what you'll need before your chicks arrive:

- Brooder box (storage tote, kennel, box, etc.)
- Heat source + thermometer
- Bedding
- Chick starter feed
- Chick feeder & waterer
- Apple cider vinegar or probiotics
- Grit (only if feeding anything besides starter feed)
- Paper towels or puppy pads
- Notebook for tracking temperature and milestones

Coop Considerations: Think Ahead

Your chicks won't stay tiny forever. Once they're feathered, they'll need a coop—so start planning early! You don't need a luxury chicken castle, but your coop should be:

- Safe from predators
- Well-ventilated and dry
- Easy to clean
- Appropriately sized: **2–4 sq ft per chicken inside, 8–10 sq ft per chicken in the run**

Budget Tip: Check Facebook Marketplace, local garden groups, or farm auctions—people often give away old coops when upgrading.

They grow faster than you think, so it's better to plan early than scramble later.

And while you're at it, consider sizing up—even if you're starting with just a few hens. Chicken math is real. Many chicken tenders (myself included) find themselves adding more birds than originally planned. Future-proofing your coop now can save you time, money, and headaches later. We'll talk more about adding future generations in **Chapter 6**.

2

Buying Your Chicks

Once your brooder is ready, it's time for the fun part—bringing home your babies! But before you head to the farm store or click "add to cart," there are a few key decisions that will shape your entire chicken-keeping journey. Where you buy your chicks (and what kind you choose) can affect their health, temperament, egg-laying, and even how peaceful your mornings are.

Let's break it all down together.

Where to Buy

You have a few solid options for sourcing your chicks:

Farm Supply Stores

- **Pros**: Instant gratification—you can walk in and walk out with peeping chicks and all the supplies you need. No shipping stress!
- **Cons**: Limited breed variety, mixed sex unless labeled, and less information about origin or early care.

This is where many beginners (myself included!) start. It's quick, convenient, and budget-friendly.

Local Hatcheries

- A great way to support small businesses, and often allows for local pickup with less shipping stress.
- Ask questions about breed selection, health protocols, and whether they offer sexed chicks.

Online Hatcheries

- Ideal if you're picky about breed, want specific egg colors, or are ordering a larger group.
- Look for live-arrival guarantees, minimum order requirements (usually 3–15 chicks), and strong customer service.

Some trusted names:

- Meyer Hatchery
- Murray McMurray
- Cackle Hatchery
- Hoover's Hatchery

Always double-check shipping timelines and temperatures for your area. Chicks ship better in spring and early summer when it's not too cold or hot.

Choosing Breeds

This is the rabbit hole (or should I say chicken tunnel?) where things get fun.

Start by asking yourself:

Do I need cold-hardy or heat-tolerant birds?

- Cold: Buff Orpington, Australorp, Barred Rock
- Heat: Leghorn, Rhode Island Red

Do I want friendly, cuddly chickens or independent foragers?

- Friendly: Cochins, Brahmas, Orpingtons
- Foragers: Easter Egger, Speckled Sussex

What kind of eggs do I want?

- White, brown, blue, green, even pinkish!
- High-laying breeds = 250–300+ eggs/year

Am I okay with noise?

- Some hens are quieter than others. Keep that in mind for cities or close neighborhoods.

New to all this? Pick 2–3 breeds to try. You'll learn which ones you love by living with them.

Understanding Sexing Terms

"How do I avoid getting a rooster?" is the #1 question I get—and it's a fair one.

Here's what you need to know:

- **Sexed chicks** – Professionally sexed at the hatchery, labeled as female (pullets). Usually about **90% accurate**.
- **Straight run** – A 50/50 mix of males and females. Cheaper, but a gamble if you're under city noise restrictions.
- **Autosex or sex-linked breeds** – These chicks show clear gender differences at hatch, making it easier to tell who's who.

Even with sexed chicks, always be prepared for a surprise rooster or two—just part of the adventure!

City Rules & Roosters

If you live in a suburban or urban area, check the local ordinances:

- How many hens are allowed?
- Are roosters prohibited?
- Do you need a permit or registration?

Roosters are louder than most people expect—and even the "quiet" ones still crow. If you're under noise restrictions, **stick with autosexed or sex-linked pullets** to reduce your chances of heartbreak (or awkward neighbor conversations).

How Many Chicks Should You Start With?

Most first-timers do great with **4–6 chicks**. It gives you enough eggs for a household, without feeling overwhelmed. Chickens are social animals, so never start with fewer than 3—they can get lonely and stressed without a flock.

Also consider:

- Your coop and run size
- Your egg needs (they don't lay every day!)
- Zoning/HOA restrictions
- How much space and time you can realistically dedicate

🐔 *Chicken math is real.* You'll always want "just a few more." Start with a reasonable number and future-proof your coop for expansion. (We'll talk more about adding future generations in Chapter 6.)

What to Look for in Healthy Chicks

Whether you're picking them up in person or unboxing a shipment, here's what you want to see:

- Bright, clear eyes
- Fluffy, dry feathers (not matted or sticky)
- Clean vent (no crusty butts!)
- Standing and walking without wobbling
- Active, curious behavior

Avoid any chicks that seem lethargic, hunched, or have crusty eyes or vents. It's worth starting with strong, vibrant birds—it sets the tone for the whole flock.

Ready to bring those fluffballs home? In the next chapter, we'll go over exactly how to care for them in their first few weeks so you can be the best chicken tender on the block.

3

Caring for Chicks Indoors

You've brought your chicks home and set them up in the brooder—now what?

The first few weeks are the most important part of their lives. This is when you'll develop your daily rhythm, get to know your new flock, and set the foundation for healthy, happy hens. With a little consistency and care, you'll be a confident chicken tender in no time.

Establish a Daily Routine

Chicks thrive on consistency. A simple rhythm helps keep them healthy and helps you catch problems early.

Morning:

- Check brooder temperature
- Refill waterer and feeder
- Spot-clean bedding
- Quick health check (especially for signs of pasty butt)

Midday:

- Observe behavior
- Refill water if needed
- Quiet bonding time—just sit nearby and talk to them

Evening:

- Final food and water check
- Spot-clean if needed
- Lower heat source for the week (if adjusting)

Chick Behavior Basics

Healthy chicks are curious and active. You'll see them:

- Peeping and scratching
- Exploring their brooder
- Napping in fuzzy little piles

Watch for signs something's off:

- Huddling under the heat = too cold
- Avoiding heat completely = too hot
- Lethargy, closed eyes, wobbly walking = illness or stress

Temperature by Week

Chicks can't regulate their body temperature yet. Use a thermometer at chick level and adjust the heat each week:

Keep the heat source on **one side** of the brooder so chicks can move closer or farther as needed. Their behavior will tell you everything you need to know.

Week	Temp
1	95°F
2	90°F
3	85°F
4	80°F
5	75°F
6	70°F (okay to move outdoors if weather allows)

Heat Lamp vs. Brooder Plate (In Depth)

There are two main options to keep your chicks warm:

Heat Lamps:

- Inexpensive and widely available

- Gets very hot—can be a fire risk if not securely mounted
- Heats the entire brooder area, not just where chicks gather
- Constant light can **disrupt natural sleep patterns**. If you use a heat lamp, opt for a **red bulb** instead of white to minimize this effect and reduce stress.

Brooder Plates:

- Mimic a mother hen by warming chicks underneath
- **Do not get as hot as heat lamps**, and that's OK—chicks self-regulate by snuggling close or moving away
- Heat is by contact—not ambient—so the surrounding area will feel cooler
- Much safer and energy-efficient

We strongly prefer brooder plates for their safety, natural feel, and peace of mind.

Bedding Basics

- **Days 1–3**: Use puppy pads or paper towels. This helps prevent chicks from eating bedding and makes it easy to monitor droppings.
- **After Day 3**: Transition to pine shavings or hemp bedding (never cedar—it's toxic!).

Why hemp? It's more absorbent and controls odor better than pine. It's low-dust, compostable, and needs changing less often, which helps balance out the upfront cost.

Avoid:

- Slippery newspaper (can cause leg issues)
- Cedar shavings (toxic)

Watch Out for Pasty Butt

This is *the* number one health issue for baby chicks. Pasty butt happens when droppings stick to their vent and block future poops. It can be fatal if not caught early.

Check their little butts daily for the first week. If you see buildup, gently clean it with warm water and dry the area. Probiotics and clean brooder conditions can help prevent it.

Feed, Water & Grit

Chicks need constant access to clean water and **starter feed.** You can choose medicated or non-medicated feed—either is fine for most backyard flocks.

Water tips:

- Use shallow chick-sized waterers
- Add **apple cider vinegar** (1 tsp per quart) to support digestion and immunity
- Keep it clean—change daily or more often if needed

Grit:

- Not needed if they're only eating starter feed
- If you offer treats like herbs, scrambled egg, or tiny bugs, you'll need to provide **chick grit** to help them digest

Supplements & Natural Boosters

Not all necessary, but incredibly helpful:

- **Electrolytes or probiotics** – Especially in the first week or after stress (like travel)
- **Fresh herbs** – Oregano, thyme, parsley, and basil support gut health and immunity
- **Flock Well™-style blends** – Herbal mixes and prebiotics can be added to food or water for added support

Cleanliness Is Everything

Chicks poop—a lot. Keep their space clean to reduce stress and illness.

- Spot-clean **twice a day**
- Do a **full clean once a week**
- Wash waterers and feeders often
- Keep bedding dry and odor-free

Building Trust with Your Chicks

Spend quiet time nearby—read a book, listen to a podcast, or hand-feed tiny treats like scrambled egg or finely chopped herbs. The more calm time you spend around them, the more they'll bond with you.

Bonding takes time, but it's worth it. You're not just raising chickens— you're raising *your* chickens.

You're officially in chicken tender mode now 🐥. Next up? Getting them ready for the big transition to the coop.

4

Transitioning to the Coop

Your tiny chicks are growing fast, and before you know it, it's time to move them outside to their permanent home: the coop. This milestone is both exciting and a little nerve-wracking for first-time chicken tenders—but with the right prep, the transition will go smoothly.

When Are Chicks Ready?

Most chicks are ready to move outdoors around **6 to 8 weeks old**, depending on the weather and breed. Here are signs they're ready:

- Fully feathered (no more fuzzy down)
- Comfortable at room temperature (around 70°F) without a heat source
- Outgrowing the brooder (flying around, crowding, or attempting to escape)

Breed matters too—larger or cold-hardy breeds may feather out sooner, while smaller or ornamental types may take a little longer.

Preparing the Coop

Start prepping your coop a week or two before the move. Your chicks will need a space that is:

- **Secure from predators** – Use hardware cloth instead of chicken wire, bury fencing to deter diggers, and add secure latches on doors and windows.
- **Dry and well-ventilated** – No standing water, no moldy bedding, and good airflow without creating drafts.
- **Clean and stocked** – Add fresh pine or hemp bedding, chick-friendly feeders and waterers, and a low roosting bar so they can start practicing.
- **Safe outdoor access** – If they'll have a run, make sure it's fully enclosed and shaded.

If possible, **introduce them gradually** by letting them explore the coop during warm afternoons and bringing them back inside at night for a few days. This helps them get comfortable without overwhelming them.

Watch the Weather

If **nighttime temps are still dipping below 60°F**, you have two choices:

- Use a **brooder plate** in the coop for another week or two
- Bring chicks inside at night and take them out during warm, sunny days

Gradual exposure to outdoor sights, sounds, and weather builds confidence and reduces the risk of chilling.

Feed Transition

Around this age, your chicks should start switching from starter feed to grower feed.

Here's how to do it:

- Mix starter and grower feed **50/50 for about 7–10 days**
- Fully transition to grower feed by week 9–10
- Don't switch to layer feed until the **first egg appears**

Continue to offer:

- Fresh, clean water at all times
- Chick grit (especially if they're eating treats or foraging)
- Optional: Herbal supplements like oregano or garlic powder to support immunity

Minimize Stress

Moving is a big deal—even for chickens. Here are a few tips to make it easier:

- **Move them during the day**, ideally in the morning or early afternoon
- **Stay nearby** for the first few hours so they feel secure
- **Give them time to explore** their new environment without overwhelming stimulation
- **Don't introduce new flock members yet**—let them settle first
- **Avoid big changes** like new treats, toys, or rearranging the coop in the first few days

That first night might feel a little uneasy for you and them, but trust that they'll settle in quickly. Chickens are creatures of habit, and with a clean, safe, and cozy space, they'll feel at home in no time.

This stage is when their personalities really shine—and you start to feel the full joy of chicken keeping. You did it, Chicken Tender. Let's talk eggs next!

5

When to Expect Eggs

You've raised your flock from fuzzy chicks to feathered teenagers, and now it's time for the ultimate reward—fresh eggs! But when do they arrive? What should you expect? And how can you help your girls lay consistently and confidently?

Let's break it down.

When Do Chickens Start Laying?

Most hens begin laying between **18 and 24 weeks old**—roughly 4.5 to 6 months. But there's a lot of variation depending on:

- **Breed** – Early layers like ISA Browns and Leghorns may start at 16–18 weeks. Heavier breeds like Orpingtons, Brahmas, and Cochins may not lay until 24–28 weeks.
- **Season** – If your hens hit maturity in fall or winter, they may delay laying until days get longer in spring. Chickens need about **14 hours of daylight** to trigger the laying cycle.
- **Nutrition & Environment** – A clean, calm coop, high-quality feed, and minimal stress help ensure timely, consistent laying.

Signs Eggs Are Coming

Here's what to watch for:

- **Bright red combs and wattles** – These enlarge and deepen in color just before laying starts.
- **Submissive squatting** – Hens may crouch down when you approach, signaling sexual maturity.
- **Increased vocalizing** – They may cluck or sing their "egg song" even before they lay.
- **Nesting box exploration** – Scratching, rearranging bedding, or hanging out in the boxes is a sure sign eggs are coming soon.

It's egg time, baby.

First Eggs: What to Expect

The first eggs—called **pullet eggs**—are often:

- Small
- Misshapen
- Have fragile or rubbery shells
- Laid on the floor instead of in the box

Don't worry—this is completely normal. Their bodies are learning the routine, and within a few weeks, you'll get more consistent, regular eggs.

Nesting Boxes on a Budget

You don't need fancy nesting boxes to keep your hens happy—just something **cozy, private, and elevated off the ground**. Here are some budget-friendly options:

- Plastic bins or milk crates turned sideways
- 5-gallon buckets laid on their side (secure them so they don't roll)
- Repurposed wooden drawers or crates

Bedding: Line with straw, **pine shavings**, or **hemp bedding** for padding. Hemp is more absorbent and offers better odor control, which means you'll need to change it less often.

Bonus Tip: Sprinkle in calming **herbs** like lavender, mint, or chamomile. These help deter pests and create a soothing environment for your girls.

Plan for **1 nesting box per 3–4 hens**—though they'll probably all still pick the same one anyway. Chicken logic.

Supporting Strong Shells

As laying ramps up, your hens will need more calcium to produce strong eggshells. Here's how to help:

- Offer **crushed oyster shell** or **baked eggshells** in a separate container (don't mix into feed)
- Make sure they have access to **clean water** at all times
- Avoid giving too many treats that dilute their balanced feed

Collecting & Storing Eggs

- **Collect eggs daily** to keep them clean and reduce the chance of broken or frozen eggs (in winter).
- If a hen goes broody and refuses to leave the nest, daily collection helps prevent that instinct from sticking.
- **Storage tip:** Fresh, unwashed eggs can sit on the **counter for up to 2 weeks**. If you **wash them**, they'll need to go in the **fridge right away**.
- Always store eggs **pointy side down**—this helps keep the yolk centered and extends freshness.

Your hens are officially laying—and you're officially a full-fledged chicken tender. 🐔🥚💖

6

Flock Planning for Long-Term Success

By now, your chickens are happily laying, and you're enjoying the fruits of your chicken-tender labor. But keeping a thriving flock isn't just about the first season—it's about planning for the long haul. With a bit of strategy, you can ensure a steady supply of eggs, happy hens, and a sustainable rhythm for years to come.

How Many Chickens Do You Really Need?

Start by considering your egg needs, space, and goals. Most hens lay 4–6 eggs per week at peak production. Here's a simple guide:

- **Solo or couple:** 3–4 hens
- **Family of 4:** 5–6 hens
- **Eggs for selling or sharing:** 8–12+ hens

More hens mean more eggs—but also more feed, more mess, and more care. Be realistic about how many you can comfortably support.

And remember: **chicken math is real.** That innocent "I'll just get four" often turns into twelve by the end of the year. You've been warned.

Understanding the Laying Cycle

Hens typically start laying between 18 and 24 weeks old and hit their peak around 1–2 years of age. After that:

- **Year 1:** Full production
- **Year 2:** Slight decline (~80–90% of year one)
- **Year 3+:** Continued tapering—some may stop, others may lay occasionally

While they may slow down, older hens still play a valuable role in your flock.

What Happens When They Stop Laying?

You have options, and it's best to decide early what your philosophy will be. Some people keep hens forever; others rehome or rotate. There's no wrong answer—just make a plan.

Here are some ways older hens can still contribute:

- **Bug patrol:** They're excellent foragers and compost helpers.
- **Broody mamas:** Older hens often go broody and make incredible moms. With a rooster, you can hatch your own chicks. Or, give a broody hen fertilized eggs (purchased online or locally) and let her do the work—no brooder required.
- **Garden crew:** Retired hens are great in garden beds—scratching, tilling, and fertilizing as they go.

Staggering Ages for Year-Round Eggs

To avoid a sudden drop in egg production as your first flock ages, add new chicks every 12–18 months. This keeps your flock diversified and your egg basket full:

- Continuous egg supply
- Easier integration with similar-aged birds
- Balanced flock dynamics and fewer medical issues all at once

Think of it like rotating crops—except they cluck.

Raising Future Generations

If you're planning to hatch your own chicks, there are a few ways to go:

- **Broody hen route:** She handles everything—incubation, hatching, and raising. You get adorable fluffballs without lifting a finger.
- **Incubator method:** Great if you want control or don't have a broody hen.
- **Buy fertilized eggs:** Cheaper than day-old chicks, easier to ship, and perfect for hatching at home.

Heads-up: You'll almost certainly get some roosters in the mix, so make sure you have a plan for them (rehoming, separate housing, etc.).

Smart Flock Expansion Tips

When adding to your flock:

- **Quarantine newcomers** for at least two weeks

- Use a **see-but-don't-touch** method for introductions
- Expect a **pecking order shuffle**—totally normal, but monitor for bullying

Budgeting for the Long Haul

Chickens are low-maintenance, but they're not zero-maintenance. Plan for:

- Feed
- Bedding
- Supplements
- Coop repairs and upgrades
- Occasional vet care (rare, but it happens)

Being proactive saves money, time, and stress down the road.

Budget Hack: Find Local Feed Sources

One of the best ways we've saved on feed is by sourcing it locally. We found a nearby farm that produces high-quality, organic feed at nearly half the price of name-brand options at big box stores. You'd be surprised how many hidden gems are out there if you're willing to ask around or attend local homesteading expos and farm shows. These events are great for making connections, learning new skills, and supporting fellow small-scale producers. It's a win-win.

Budget Hack: Ferment Their Feed

Once your flock transitions to grower feed, you can also begin **fermenting** their food. It not only stretches your feed farther—cutting costs—

but it also makes the nutrients more bioavailable, improves gut health, and reduces waste.

Here's how to do it:

1. **Use pelleted or mash feed** (do *not* ferment crumble—it turns into a soupy mess).
2. Add the feed to a clean bucket or container.
3. Cover with water until the feed is fully submerged, plus about an inch.
4. Let it sit in a **cool, dark place** for **2–3 days**, stirring once or twice daily.
5. When you see bubbles and a slightly tangy smell, it's ready to serve.
6. Scoop out and feed what they'll eat in about an hour. *No worries— they'll usually devour it like it's chicken candy.*
7. If you consistently have leftover fermented feed, you're feeding too much at once. Offer it 1–2 times a day, or let them free-range and supplement with ferment in smaller amounts.

Tip: I always keep **dry, unfermented feed available free-choice** so they can snack throughout the day and maintain a healthy balance.

With thoughtful flock planning, your hens will keep you in eggs, compost, and chicken joy for years. Whether you raise your own replacements or buy new chicks every few seasons, your future self (and future breakfasts) will thank you.

7

Health Checks & Common Ailments

Backyard chickens are surprisingly hardy, but they're not invincible—especially during that first year. A little daily observation and a few basic supplies can go a long way in keeping your flock healthy and preventing most problems before they start.

Let's walk through what to look for, how to handle the most common issues, and how to build a proactive wellness routine.

Daily Wellness Checks

You don't need to be a vet—just a mindful observer. A quick once-over every morning and evening makes a world of difference. Watch for:

- **Bright eyes** – Open, alert, and free of crustiness or bubbles
- **Clean feathers** – No sudden loss, especially around the vent or neck
- **Comb and wattles** – Vibrant, smooth, and not pale or shriveled
- **Normal posture and movement** – No limping, hunching, or puffed-up isolation

- **Vent area** – Clean and dry (chicks: watch for pasty butt!)
- **Feet and legs** – No swelling, sores, or raised scales
- **Behavior** – Active, curious, eating, and dust bathing

If something feels "off," it probably is. Trust your chicken tender instincts.

Yes, You'll Become a Poop Inspector

Chicken droppings are a surprisingly helpful health indicator.

- **Normal poop** changes throughout the day, especially with diet.
- **Green or watery droppings** may signal stress or poor nutrition.
- **Bloody stools** (especially in chicks) may indicate **coccidiosis**.
- **Persistent diarrhea** raises risk of dehydration and illness.

Using puppy pads or paper towels during the chick stage helps you monitor more easily. Dry bedding = healthy chicks.

Common Ailments & What to Do

Here are the basics every chicken tender should know:

1. Pasty Butt (Chicks Only)

Droppings harden and block the vent—can be fatal if not treated.

- **Signs:** Poop crust on the vent
- **Fix:** Gently wipe with warm water, pat dry. Add probiotics or apple cider vinegar to water for prevention.

HEALTH CHECKS & COMMON AILMENTS

2. Coccidiosis (Chicks & Young Birds)
A parasitic infection of the intestinal lining.

- **Signs:** Lethargy, blood in stool, puffed posture
- **Fix:** Add **Corid (amprolium)** to water immediately. Don't wait—this spreads fast.

3. Mites & Lice
Tiny parasites that cause irritation and feather loss.

- **Signs:** Feather loss, pale combs, scratching, red or scabby skin
- **Fix:** Deep clean the coop. Dust with wood ash or **herbal poultry dust**. Avoid or minimize DE (diatomaceous earth)—it's effective but controversial due to respiratory risks.

Safer alternatives include:

- Neem-based sprays
- Dried herbs like lavender, mint, and eucalyptus
- Daily access to dust baths (wood ash, sand, dried herbs)

4. Respiratory Infections
Contagious and sometimes chronic.

- **Signs:** Sneezing, eye bubbles, nasal discharge, raspy breathing
- **Fix:** Isolate the bird. Add oregano or thyme to water/feed. If symptoms worsen, call a vet. Clean coop and boost ventilation.

5. **Bumblefoot**
An infection caused by a cut or puncture in the foot.

- **Signs:** Limping, swollen or scabby foot pad
- **Fix:** Soak in Epsom salt water, apply antibacterial ointment. In advanced cases, vet care may be needed.

Herbal & Natural Support

Building health from the inside out is a key part of our philosophy. Herbs are not a cure-all—but they're a powerful long-term support strategy.

Here's our core rotation:

- **Oregano:** Gut + respiratory support
- **Thyme:** Immune-boosting + antimicrobial
- **Mint:** Cooling and pest-repelling
- **Garlic:** Immune support, parasite deterrent
- **Chamomile:** Calming + anti-inflammatory
- **Lavender:** Soothes stress, deters mites
- **Calendula:** Skin healing + anti-fungal
- **Parsley:** Vitamin-rich, great for growing chicks
- **Apple Cider Vinegar:** Improves digestion (1 tsp per quart of water, 2–3x per week)

How to Use Herbs:

- Mix in feed or sprinkle in bedding
- Add to nesting boxes
- Brew into a weak "herbal tea" for water
- Offer free-choice for chickens to self-select (they often know what

they need)

Rotate weekly or monthly based on the season, and observe what your flock gravitates toward.

Natural First Aid Kit Essentials

Stock a basic kit so you're not scrambling in an emergency:

- **Epsom salt** (for soaks)
- **Apple cider vinegar**
- **Triple antibiotic ointment** (no pain reliever!)
- **Electrolytes or Nutri-Drench**
- **Saline solution** (for flushing eyes or wounds)
- **Clean rags/gauze**
- **Corid (amprolium)**
- **Natural wound spray**
- **Poultry probiotics**
- **A dog crate or tote for isolation**

Having supplies on hand buys you time and peace of mind.

When to Call a Vet

You can handle most things yourself, but don't hesitate to get help when:

- A chicken is very lethargic and not eating or drinking
- Respiratory symptoms worsen despite care
- A wound shows pus, swelling, or bone exposure
- You aren't sure what's going on and need expert eyes

Many vets are now open to backyard poultry consultations—or find a local poultry group online for support and referrals.

With a little prevention, a good routine, and a watchful eye, your flock can thrive for years. You don't have to be perfect—you just have to be present.

8

Keep Growing With Your Flock

You did it, chicken tender! Whether you're still setting up your brooder or collecting a rainbow of fresh eggs each morning, you now have the foundational knowledge to raise healthy, happy backyard chickens—on a budget and with confidence.

But here's the thing: **this is just the beginning**.

Raising chickens isn't just about fresh eggs or cute clucks (though those are definite perks). It's about reconnecting with the rhythms of nature, learning to care for something beyond yourself, and finding unexpected joy in the little things—like a hen's happy dust bath or that first surprise egg in the nesting box.

Chickens often become the gateway to something more. They spark curiosity. Suddenly, you're composting, planting herbs, experimenting with sourdough, or dreaming about goats. You find yourself craving more freedom, more connection, and more intention in how you live and what you consume.

And yes, you'll stumble. You'll make mistakes. You'll second-guess and Google things at 2 a.m. But the beauty of this journey is that you learn by doing—and there's no "right" way to do it. If you're showing up, paying attention, and doing your best, you're doing just fine.

So keep growing. Keep asking questions. Keep finding your rhythm.

Whether you're raising a few hens in a tiny urban backyard or building your dream homestead out in the country, you're part of a beautiful movement of people choosing to live more rooted, more intentionally, and a little closer to the land.

Follow My Homesteading Journey

If this book helped you even a little, I'd love to stay connected. Over at **Rooted in Modern Life**, I share real-life homesteading lessons, chicken-keeping tips, garden inspiration, herbal remedies, cozy recipes, and the occasional chicken fail (because we all have them!).

Come say hi:

- **Instagram:** @rootedinmodernlife
- **YouTube:** Rooted in Modern Life
- **TikTok:** @rootedinmodernlife
- **Facebook**: Rooted in Modern Life
- **Website & Blog:** RootedinModernLife.com

Chicken Keeping Tools & Supplies

- **Brooder Setup:** Storage bin, cardboard box, or pop-up kennel
- **Heat Source:** Brooder plate (preferred) or a red-bulb heat lamp
- **Feeder & Waterer:** Chick-safe, easy to clean
- **Bedding:** Pine shavings or hemp
- **Supplements:** Probiotics, electrolytes, apple cider vinegar, oyster shell, grit
- **Egg Basket or Apron:** Trust me—you'll thank yourself
- **Herbs:** Oregano, thyme, mint, lavender, chamomile, calendula

Final Tips Before You Go

- Start small and grow your confidence alongside your flock.
- Observe your birds—they'll show you what they need.
- Trust your gut. If something seems off, it usually is.
- Chicken math is real. You've been warned.

If You Enjoyed This Book...

Please consider leaving a quick review on Amazon. Reviews help new readers find this resource and support independent creators like me. It only takes a minute—and it truly makes a huge difference.

Thank you for letting me be a small part of your chicken-keeping adventure. Here's to fresh eggs, happy hens, and a life rooted in something real.

9

Resources

Additional Resources & Learning Hubs

Here are a few of my favorite go-to sources for continued learning and community support:

- **Storey's Guide to Raising Chickens** – Gail Damerow
- **The Chicken Health Handbook** – Gail Damerow
- **Fresh Eggs Daily** – Lisa Steele
- **The Chicken Chick Blog** – the-chicken-chick.com
- **Backyard Chickens Forum** – backyardchickens.com
- **Flock Well™** – Herbal support for happy hens, launching soon at RootedinModernLife.com

Cited & Referenced Sources

Damerow, G. (2010). *Storey's Guide to Raising Chickens* (3rd ed.). Storey Publishing.

Damerow, G. (2015). *The Chicken Health Handbook* (2nd ed.). Storey Publishing.

Steele, L. (2013). *Fresh Eggs Daily: Raising Happy, Healthy Chickens Naturally.* St. Lynn's Press.

Raney, M. (Host). (2016–present). *Homestead Rescue* [TV series]. All3Media America; Discovery Channel.

U.S. Department of Agriculture. (n.d.). *Chick care basics.* Retrieved from https://www.usda.gov

Rooted in Modern Life. (2025). *Backyard chicken care blog series.* Retrieved from https://www.rootedinmodernlife.com

Flock Well™. (2025). *Herbal chicken health and natural support research trials.* Unpublished data.

About the Author

Ginger Allen is a real estate broker turned homesteader, chicken tender, and passionate advocate for living a rooted, intentional life. After years of dreaming (and researching herself into a full-on analysis paralysis spiral), she and her husband dove headfirst into backyard chicken keeping in 2024—on a budget, with zero prior experience, and a whole lot of heart.

What started as a few chicks in a pop-up dog kennel quickly blossomed into a full-blown homestead lifestyle. Now living on acreage in the Oklahoma countryside, Ginger shares her journey—flocks, gardens, sourdough fails, and all—through her platform, **Rooted in Modern Life**.

She believes self-sufficiency is for everyone, whether you're on a farm or in a city backyard, and she's here to prove that you don't need a fortune or perfection to get started—just curiosity, courage, and maybe a few chickens.

You can follow Ginger's homestead adventures on Instagram, TikTok, YouTube, and Facebook @rootedinmodernlife or visit her website at www.rootedinmodernlife.com.

You can connect with me on:
- https://www.rootedinmodernlife.com
- https://www.facebook.com/rootedinmodernlife
- https://www.instagram.com/rootedinmodernlife
- https://www.youtube.com/@rootedinmodernlife
- https://www.tiktok.com/@rootedinmodernlife

Made in the USA
Columbia, SC
11 April 2025